From Detroit to Micros

The Energetic Rise of Steve Ballmer

Biography of Steve Ballmer

Copyright

2024 All rights reserved
Richard Brownfield

Table of Contents

Chapter 1. Introduction: The Man Behind the Microsoft Empire

Chapter 2. Childhood and Early Life: The Making of a Tech Titan

Chapter 3: Joining Microsoft: Ballmer's Ascension to Power

Chapter 4. The Gates-Ballmer Era: The Golden Age of Microsoft

Chapter 5: Challenges and Controversies: Ballmer's Leadership Style Examined

Chapter 6. Post-Microsoft Career: A New Chapter Begins

Steve Ballmer Net Worth

Steve Ballmer Contributions to Philanthropy

Chapter 7. Philanthropy and Personal Life: Behind the Scenes of Steve Ballmer's Private World

Chapter 8. Legacy and Impact: Ballmer's Contributions to the Tech Industry and Beyond

Chapter 9. Conclusion: Lessons Learned from the Life of Steve Ballmer

Chapter 1. Introduction: The Man Behind the Microsoft Empire

Steve Ballmer's name is synonymous with Microsoft, the tech behemoth he helped grow into an empire during his term as CEO. For more than a decade, Ballmer led one of the world's most influential and successful firms, profoundly altering the future of technology and business.

But who is the man behind the Microsoft empire? What inspires, motivates, and drives him to greatness? To comprehend Ballmer's story, we must travel back to his childhood and follow him from a young boy with enormous goals to one of the most prominent and important figures in the computing world.

Ballmer showed a great ability for math and science from an early age, excelling in his courses and exhibiting a significant interest in technology. He was enthralled by the growing subject of computer science and saw its enormous potential to revolutionize the world. As he grew older, his interest in technology grew stronger, and he began to fantasize about founding his own company and leaving his mark on the world.

After finishing his studies at Harvard, Ballmer joined Microsoft as its first business manager, working closely with co-founder Bill Gates to help the company grow and broaden its reach. He ascended through the ranks to become one of Gates' closest confidants and most valued advisors, playing a significant role in determining the company's strategy and direction.

But it wasn't until Ballmer took over as CEO in 2000 that he truly came into his own, leading Microsoft through some of its most difficult and revolutionary years. Under his leadership, the business overcame tough competition from rivals such as Google and Apple, expanded into new markets and industries, and continued to innovate and push the frontiers of what was possible with technology.

Throughout it all, Ballmer remained strongly committed to Microsoft's goal and vision, working diligently to ensure that the business remained faithful to its basic beliefs and ideals. He was recognized for his enthusiastic and energetic leadership style, frequently making stirring speeches and rallying cries that energized his staff and rallied the company's fans.

However, Ballmer's legacy extends far beyond his time at Microsoft. In the years since stepping down as CEO, he has remained a strong player in the internet industry and beyond, lending his wealth and influence to a variety of causes and initiatives. From philanthropy to education to sports, Ballmer has established himself as a visionary leader and ardent advocate for change.

In this chapter, we will look at Steve Ballmer's life and career, from his early years as a brilliant and ambitious young man to his climb to power at Microsoft and beyond. We'll look at his leadership style, his skills and faults, and the impact he's had on the IT industry and the globe at large. Through it all, we will witness the man behind the Microsoft empire, a complicated and varied figure whose impact continues to inspire and affect us today.

Chapter 2. Childhood and Early Life: The Making of a Tech Titan

Steve Ballmer is a household name in the IT business. The former Microsoft CEO is well-known for his dynamic leadership style, inventive vision, and enormous wealth. Ballmer was a little boy growing up in Detroit, Michigan, before becoming a tech tycoon.

Early Childhood and Adolescence

Steve Ballmer was born in Detroit, Michigan, on March 24, 1956. Frederic Henry Ballmer, a Swiss immigrant who worked as a manager at Ford Motor Company, was his father. Beatrice Dworkin Ballmer, his mother, was a Jewish immigrant from Belarus who worked as a housekeeper.

Ballmer grew up in Farmington Hills, Michigan, an upscale suburb, and attended Detroit Country Day School. He was noted as a child for his great energy and competitive nature. He was a member of the high school basketball team and an active debater.

Ballmer was raised by parents who instilled in him a strong work ethic and a desire to learn. They encouraged him to pursue his passions and to strive for greatness at all times. This early encouragement shaped Ballmer's personality and set him on the route to success.

Ballmer entered Harvard University in 1973 to study mathematics and economics. He was a member of Harvard's varsity football and lacrosse teams. He also oversaw the school's basketball squad.

Ballmer met Bill Gates, who was also a student at Harvard, during his stay there. They became friends and went on to build one of the most successful businesses in history.

Career Starts

Ballmer began his career with Procter & Gamble as an associate product manager after graduating from Harvard in 1977. He rapidly realized that he wanted to work in technology and enrolled in the MBA program at Stanford University.

While at Stanford, Ballmer interned for Microsoft, which was formed in 1975 by his buddy Bill Gates. Ballmer joined Microsoft as the company's 30th employee after earning his MBA in 1980.

Microsoft was still a small company that focused on building software for personal computers at the time. But Ballmer recognized the company's potential for development and expansion, and he swiftly rose to become one of its most influential leaders.

Ascension to fame

Ballmer's meteoric rise began in the early 1990s, when he was named executive vice president of sales and support at Microsoft. In this capacity, he was in charge of the company's efforts to grow into new markets and develop new products.

Ballmer's work in the development of Windows, Microsoft's main operating system, was one of his most significant achievements to the corporation. He was instrumental in the development of Windows 95, which went on to become one of the most successful software programs in history.

Ballmer succeeded Bill Gates as CEO of Microsoft in 2000. As CEO, he oversaw some of the most major advances in the company's history, including the introduction of Xbox and Microsoft Office.

Ballmer was noted for his enthusiastic and passionate leadership style, sometimes shouting and bouncing about on stage at company events. He was also well-known for his competitive nature and commitment to innovation.

Microsoft continues to thrive and expand under Ballmer's leadership. The corporation introduced new products and services, purchased other businesses, and entered new markets. Ballmer was acclaimed for his vision and abilities to drive company innovation.

Retirement and Giving

After 34 years with Microsoft, Ballmer announced his retirement in 2014. He died with a net worth of more than $20 billion, making him one of the world's richest people.

After his retirement, Ballmer focused on philanthropy. His wife, Connie, and he founded the Ballmer Group, a nonprofit organization focused to enhancing economic mobility for children and families.

The Ballmer Group has made significant investments in early childhood education and has pledged a $1 billion donation over the next ten years. In addition, Ballmer has made major contributions to healthcare research, including a $50 million gift to the

Fred Hutchinson Cancer Research Center in 2018.

Chapter 3: Joining Microsoft: Ballmer's Ascension to Power

Ballmer was recognized for his passionate and energetic leadership style, often making stirring speeches and rallying cries that energized his staff and rallied the company's supporters.

But Ballmer's time at Microsoft was not without its difficulties. The company drew criticism for its business methods, particularly in the areas of antitrust and privacy. Ballmer was also chastised for how he handled important strategic decisions, notably as the unsuccessful acquisition of Yahoo in 2008.

Despite these difficulties, Ballmer remained committed to Microsoft and its goal. He continued to manage the company through difficult times, constantly seeking to adhere to its essential ideals and beliefs. He stepped down as CEO of Microsoft in 2014, but his legacy at Microsoft and in the computer industry as a whole lives on.

Apart from Microsoft

Aside from his work at Microsoft, Ballmer has become a notable figure in philanthropy and public service. He and his wife, Connie, have given millions of dollars to a variety of causes, including education, healthcare, and social justice. In 2018, Ballmer founded USAFacts, a non-profit organization dedicated to provide fair statistics and analysis on government spending and performance.

Chapter 4. The Gates-Ballmer Era: The Golden Age of Microsoft

They were recognized for their passionate and energetic leadership style, often making stirring speeches and rallying cries that energized their staff and rallied the company's fans.

The Legacy of the Gates-Ballmer Era

Microsoft today is a completely different company than it was during the Gates-Ballmer era. Gates has stepped down from his position at the corporation, focusing instead on philanthropy and other projects. Ballmer has also moved on, pursuing new endeavors such as his ownership of the Los Angeles Clippers basketball franchise.

But the legacy of the Gates-Ballmer era lingers on. Microsoft is one of the world's most renowned companies, with a long history of innovation and success. Its products are utilized by billions of people worldwide, and its impact reaches far beyond the realm of computing.

The Gates-Ballmer era was a golden age for Microsoft, when two visionary visionaries came together to develop a corporation that altered the globe. Their legacy continues to inspire and impact the tech industry today, reminding us of the power of innovation, determination, and teamwork.

Chapter 5: Challenges and Controversies: Ballmer's Leadership Style Examined

Steve Ballmer, who once electrified boardrooms with his lunges and roars, left Microsoft as a behemoth, with its revenue quadrupling and Windows entrenched in homes and businesses around the world. Nonetheless, his legacy is a battleground, carved with both successes and setbacks. His leadership, a strong cocktail of passion, energy, and occasional turpitude, catapulted Microsoft to unprecedented heights while also inviting scrutiny and controversy.

This contagious zeal produced unmistakable results. Microsoft grew from a minor software provider to a tech powerhouse under Ballmer's leadership. When Windows XP was released in 2001, it became a cultural phenomenon, with millions of workstations sporting green hills and blue skies. The Xbox, a brave push into console gaming, challenged Sony's stronghold with the PlayStation. Ballmer, ever the salesperson, even persuaded the Pentagon to switch from Apple to Windows computers, a multibillion-dollar coup.

However, there were certain drawbacks to Ballmer's leadership. While inspiring, his zeal might verge on aggressiveness. Critics dubbed him a bully who was ready to dismiss and berate others. His steadfast confidence in Windows blinded him to the burgeoning mobile revolution, with the iPhone serving as a phantom limb he disregarded as a "cute toy." While the mobile world moved beneath his feet, Ballmer invested billions of dollars into unsuccessful enterprises like Zune and Windows Phone.

Internally, Ballmer's tenure was typified by a fearful and micromanaging mentality. Employees were frightened to innovate because of his tantrums. Bureaucracy suffocated creativity, suffocating Microsoft's entrepreneurial spirit. Ballmer, the consummate marketer, struggled to understand the language of Silicon Valley's "cool kids," his attempts at hipness frequently landing with an unpleasant thud.

But portraying Ballmer only as a clumsy monarch in a collapsing Microsoft empire would be unfair. He acknowledged his flaws and appointed Satya Nadella, a soft-spoken engineer, as his replacement. Nadella's data-driven strategy, which contrasted sharply with Ballmer's emotive firebrand, ushered in a new era of cloud computing and mobile concentration, bringing Microsoft back from the verge of bankruptcy.

As a result, Ballmer's legacy is a tapestry of triumphs and tragedies, strong strokes of vision and exasperating blind spots. He was a leader who "danced on the edge," as he put it, driving Microsoft to dizzying heights while occasionally tripping. He was a man of contradictions: a salesman who established an empire, a cheerleader who instilled dread, and a visionary who failed to predict the future. Finally, Steve Ballmer's biography serves as a reminder that even the most zealous leaders have enduring legacies, testaments to both the genius and fallibility of the human spirit.

His story is about the hazards and promises of leadership, the fine line between conviction and delusion, the human cost of ambition, and the enduring appeal of redemption, not just Microsoft. Steve Ballmer, the man who once screamed through boardrooms, may have stepped down from the stage, but his voice, a mix of triumph and sorrow, still lingers in the halls of tech history, a cautionary tale and an inspiring epic for future leaders.

The second act of Ballmer's leadership, defined by wasted chances and internal strife, calls for more investigation. While Windows commanded the desktop, the tech tectonic plates beneath him were changing. Apple, once dismissed as a marginal company, stormed forward with the iPod and iPhone, rewriting the digital consumption norms. Google, the modest search engine, has evolved into an innovation behemoth, with its Android operating system dominating the mobile world that Ballmer has persistently disregarded.

Blind spots were not Ballmer's only flaw. Fear and mistrust had taken root within the organization. The "stack ranking" system, which pitted staff against one another in a yearly performance evaluation and labeled a specific number of employees as "losers," encouraged harsh rivalry and hindered collaboration. Bureaucracy and a risk-averse environment stunted innovation. Ballmer, ever the marketer, battled to keep up with Silicon Valley's shifting tides. His attempts to entice younger audiences with clumsy dancing moves and weird lingo were met with scoffs rather than cheers.

Despite this, glimmerings of self-awareness and path correction appeared from the darkness. Recognizing the need for transformation, Ballmer made a series of acquisitions, including LinkedIn for its professional network and Skype for its communication capabilities. He named Satya Nadella as his successor, a quiet but data-driven leader who signals a change toward a more analytical and collaborative approach. It was a risk, an unspoken admission that his own strengths had become limits.

The entrance of Nadella represented a seismic upheaval. Windows, long the royal gem, has been dethroned, and its focus has been reduced to essential functionality. Microsoft ultimately recognized mobile as the elephant in the room, adopting Android and developing its own Surface line of devices. Nadella, the antithesis of Ballmer's noisy flair, led with quiet confidence and data-driven judgments, building a long-missing culture of cooperation and invention.

Ballmer's story is thus one of victory and tragedy, a Shakespearean tragedy performed on the digital stage. He was the salesperson who created an empire, the cheerleader who instilled fear, and the visionary who failed to see the future. His legacy is a complex tapestry woven with powerful strokes of brilliance and maddening blind spots, rather than one of overwhelming success. He propelled Microsoft to unfathomable heights, leaving behind a business four times the size of the one he inherited. His tenure, however, also left a lengthy shadow of wasted opportunities and suffocating bureaucracy, serving as a cautionary tale for future leaders wrestling with the hazards and promises of ambition.

So, where does Ballmer rank among the technology titans? He wasn't the contemplative architect Gates or the extroverted showman Jobs. He was, arguably, considerably more human: a passionate leader with weaknesses and blind spots who skated on the verge of greatness, driving his organization to greatness while occasionally stumbling. His story serves as a reminder that even the brightest minds can make mistakes, that leadership is a fine line between conviction and delusion, and that forgiveness is always a possibility, even in the harsh world of technology.

Chapter 6. Post-Microsoft Career: A New Chapter Begins

After 14 years as CEO of Microsoft, Steve Ballmer stepped down in 2014. Many questioned what would happen next for the IT industry veteran, but Ballmer was fast to start a new chapter in his career. In this biography, we'll look at Ballmer's post-Microsoft career and the impact he's had on the business world after leaving the software behemoth.

LA Clippers

One of the first big acts Ballmer made after leaving Microsoft was the $2 billion purchase of the Los Angeles Clippers basketball team. Many people were startled by this move because Ballmer was not renowned for his passion in sports. However, he saw an opportunity to invest in a team that had been mired in controversy and legal troubles and believed that he could turn things around.

The Clippers have become one of the most successful teams in the NBA because of Ballmer's leadership. He has invested extensively in the team's facilities and infrastructure, including a new training complex and arena. He has also sought to improve the team's culture and reputation, focusing on transparency and responsibility. Beyond basketball, Ballmer has utilized his Clippers ownership to promote social justice and philanthropy. He has given millions of dollars to different causes, including education, healthcare, and technology.

USAFacts

In 2017, Ballmer established USAFacts, a non-profit company dedicated to delivering accurate and comprehensive data on government spending and performance. Ballmer was frustrated by the lack of transparency and accountability in government, which inspired the creation of USAFacts.

USA Facts compiles data from many government sources and provides it in an easy-to-understand style. The organization's website contains data on government revenue and spending, as well as data on numerous social and economic topics. USAFacts is nonpartisan and does not advocate for any certain policy or political agenda.

Ballmer has stated that the purpose of USAFacts is to provide citizens with the information they need to make educated decisions regarding government policy. He believes that transparency and accountability are necessary for a healthy democracy and that USAFacts may help to promote these values.

Initiatives for Civic Participation

In addition to his work with the Clippers and USAFacts, Ballmer has been involved in a variety of civic efforts. He has donated millions of dollars to organizations that promote education, healthcare, and social justice. He has also participated in initiatives to promote economic development and job creation in the United States.

The Ballmer Group, a nonprofit organization he co-founded with his wife, Connie, is one of Ballmer's most major civic projects. The Ballmer Group works to increase economic mobility and opportunity for children and families in the United States. The organization supports a wide range of programs and projects, including early childhood education, job development, and affordable housing.

The Ballmer Group has also been involved in the fight against the COVID-19 pandemic. In 2020, the organization will provide $25 million to promote virus research and development of therapies and vaccinations.

Biography of Steve Ballmer

Steve Ballmer Net Worth

The Unwavering CEO: A Portrait of Steve Ballmer's Billion-Dollar Legacy

Steve Ballmer is one of our generation's most successful and prominent corporate CEOs. As Microsoft's previous CEO, he was instrumental in defining the technology industry and transforming how we live and work. But, in addition to his professional accomplishments, Ballmer is well-known for his vast fortune and charitable contributions. In this article, we'll look at Steve Ballmer's net worth in depth, investigating how he got his fortune, how he manages his wealth, and how he uses his resources to make a positive impact on the world.

Early Career and Ascension to Notoriety

Before delving into Ballmer's net worth, it's essential to understand his early career and meteoric ascent to stardom. Ballmer joined Microsoft as the company's 30th employee in 1980, shortly after graduating from Stanford University's MBA program. He quickly progressed through the ranks, eventually becoming the company's first business manager and serving as CEO from 2000 to 2014.

During his time as CEO, Ballmer oversaw some of Microsoft's most major achievements, such as the introduction of Windows XP, Xbox, and Microsoft Office.

He was also instrumental in the company's expansion into new markets such as mobile devices and cloud computing.

Ballmer was known at Microsoft for his energetic and passionate leadership style. He was frequently seen shouting and jumping around on stage at company events, earning him the nickname "Monkey Boy" among some colleagues. Despite his outlandish approach, Ballmer was widely admired for his vision and commitment to innovation.

Making It Rich

So, how did Steve Ballmer become wealthy? The majority of his fortune stems from his time at Microsoft, where he amassed substantial stock and other assets. Ballmer's net worth is estimated to be $110.2 billion as of 2024, making him one of the world's wealthiest people.

Ballmer's fortune is heavily reliant on his Microsoft stock holdings. He owns about 4% of the company's outstanding shares, which are worth around $60 billion at the moment. He also has a stake in the Los Angeles Clippers, which he purchased in 2014 for $2 billion.

Aside from his stakes in Microsoft and the Los Angeles Clippers, Ballmer has made a number of other investments over the years. He announced plans to establish a new nonprofit organization aimed at improving government services in 2018. He's also invested in companies like Twitter and Airbnb.

Taking Care of His Money

How does Steve Ballmer manage his wealth with such a vast fortune at his disposal? According to reports, he manages his investments with the help of a team of financial advisors.

Ballmer has become more involved in philanthropic endeavors. He announced in 2018 that he would be donating $59 million to the University of Oregon for a new computer science building. He has also made significant contributions to other causes, such as medical research and educational initiatives.

Despite his enormous wealth, Ballmer is known to lead a modest lifestyle. He allegedly drives a Ford Fusion and lives in a modest Seattle neighborhood. He has also expressed a desire to pay higher taxes and make a greater contribution to society.

Contributions to Philanthropy

One of the most notable aspects of Steve Ballmer's fortune is his generosity. He has given millions of dollars to various causes and organizations over the years, with a special emphasis on education and healthcare.

Ballmer and his wife Connie founded the Ballmer Group, a philanthropic organization dedicated to increasing economic mobility for children and families, in 2014. The organization has made significant investments in early childhood education and has committed to donating $1 billion over the next decade.

Ballmer has also participated in a number of other charitable endeavors. He gave $10 million to the computer science department at the University of Washington in 2019. He has also made substantial contributions to medical research, including a $50 million gift to the Fred Hutchinson Cancer Research Center in 2018.

Chapter 7. Philanthropy and Personal Life: Behind the Scenes of Steve Ballmer's Private World

This is not a biography of Ballmer the executive, but rather a look at Ballmer the philanthropist, who uses his fortune to combat inequality and injustice.

His philanthropic journey was not a sudden turn, but rather an evolution woven into the fabric of his being. While Microsoft soared under his leadership, Ballmer quietly nurtured a deep empathy for those left behind by the digital revolution. He felt restless as he saw the chasm between the haves and have-nots widen. Education, he believed, was the bridge, and his first major contribution was a $50 million gift to his alma mater, the University of Oregon. This wasn't just charity; it was an investment in potential, an opportunity to equip future generations with the tools they need to navigate the ever-changing tech landscape.

But Ballmer's vision extended beyond the ivory towers. He witnessed the silent struggles of those dealing with mental health issues, particularly children. His own family's experiences with the complexities of mental health fueled his determination to address this often-ignored societal challenge. In a historic move, he donated $425 million to the University of Oregon, establishing the Ballmer Institute for Children's Behavioral Health - a beacon of hope for families dealing with anxiety, depression, and other mental health issues. It wasn't just about funding research; it was about breaking down stigmas and creating a support system in which vulnerability was seen as a strength to be embraced rather than a weakness to be avoided.

Education and mental health were only the tip of the iceberg. Ballmer's philanthropic tentacles extended into the far reaches of social justice. He addressed the economic disparities that plague communities by supporting initiatives that empower individuals and bridge the gap between potential and opportunity. He advocated for environmental causes, recognizing the delicate balance between technological advancement and ecological preservation. He even ventured into the murky waters of political reform, advocating for transparency and accountability in government through his creation, USAFacts.

His approach is as unique as his persona. Ballmer isn't one for silent donations or quiet pats on the back. He dives headfirst into the trenches, engaging with beneficiaries, challenging the status quo, and demanding measurable impact. He is not afraid to hold his own grantees accountable, pushing them to innovate and maximize the effectiveness of their programs. This hands-on approach, while occasionally ruffling feathers, ensures that his resources are more than just bandages on gaping wounds, but catalysts for long-term change.

One could argue that Ballmer's philanthropy is simply a byproduct of his enormous wealth, a noblesse oblige act expected of a billionaire. However, reducing his efforts to mere tax breaks would be a gross oversimplification. The fire in his eyes when he speaks about closing the digital divide, the empathy he exudes when discussing mental health struggles, and the tenacity he exhibits in addressing systemic injustices are not the hallmarks of a man simply fulfilling his philanthropic duty. They are the characteristics of a man who is driven by a genuine desire to make the world a better place, one impact at a time.

So, the next time you hear the name Steve Ballmer, don't just think of the booming CEO or the NBA superfan. Remember the man who fights for educational equity, promotes mental health awareness, and works to bridge the economic divide. Remember the philanthropist who uses his wealth to affect positive change rather than as a symbol of privilege. Remember Steve Ballmer, the man whose passion can be heard far beyond the boardroom and the courtside seats.

This is not the end of the story, but rather a glimpse into a chapter that is still being written. As Ballmer navigates the philanthropic landscape, one thing is certain: his impact will be measured not in dollars donated, but in lives transformed and a world made more just, one step at a time.

Chapter 8. Legacy and Impact: Ballmer's Contributions to the Tech Industry and Beyond

Steve Ballmer was a whirlwind of energy disguised as a man. His influence on the technology industry and beyond was a symphony of calculated boldness, unwavering belief, and infectious passion that redefined possibilities. His legacy can be heard in the hum of cloud servers, the rumble of Xbox controllers, and the echoes in classrooms bathed in the glow of educational software.

To say that Ballmer is a leader would be an understatement. He was a sculptor who transformed a scrappy Seattle startup into a tech behemoth that reshaped the digital landscape. He saw personal computers as more than just tools, but as gateways to individual empowerment and global connectivity. Under his leadership, Windows evolved from a niche product to a household term, democratizing access to information and revolutionizing how we work, learn, and play.

Ballmer, on the other hand, wasn't a one-trick pony. He saw the horizon before others, daring to take risks in uncharted territory. When the internet exploded in the 1990s, he didn't just dabble; he created MSN, a web portal that became a portal to the online world for millions of people. Recognizing the looming threat of free software, he spearheaded Microsoft's acquisition of LinkedIn, a strategic move that not only bolstered Microsoft's professional networking but also cemented its relevance in the age of social media.

Ballmer was unafraid of failing. Do you recall Windows Vista? Yes, it was a massive blunder, but it fueled the flames of innovation, leading to the triumphant rise of Windows 7. He recognized that even mistakes can teach valuable lessons, and his unwavering optimism propelled Microsoft through setbacks as well as triumphs.

Ballmer's vision went beyond the software behemoth. He recognized the transformative power of technology in education and led initiatives to bring computers and learning resources to underserved communities. He was an outspoken supporter of philanthropy, with his foundation addressing global health issues and empowering aspiring entrepreneurs. This was more than just corporate social responsibility; it was a genuine belief in the ability of technology to uplift and empower.

Ballmer's legacy, on the other hand, is not without complexities. His fiery passion wasn't always regarded as endearing; his detractors labeled him brash, even bombastic. But it was that intensity that drove him, pushing him to defy expectations and push the boundaries. He wasn't afraid to ruffle feathers, but beneath his fiery persona was a deep dedication to his people and his beliefs.

Steve Ballmer's story isn't just about lines of code or dollars and cents; it's about an unwavering faith in technology's transformative power. He wasn't just a CEO; he was a champion, an evangelist, a natural force who dared to dream big and push harder. His legacy is woven into the fabric of our digital lives, a testament to the man who saw computers as catalysts for a brighter future rather than tools.

So, the next time you fire up your laptop, connect with a colleague halfway around the world, or get lost in a virtual world, remember the man who helped make it all possible. Remember Steve Ballmer, the whirlwind who reshaped the world one pixel at a time.

Chapter 9. Conclusion: Lessons Learned from the Life of Steve Ballmer

Steve Ballmer's life and career have been nothing short of extraordinary. From his early days at Microsoft to his post-Microsoft initiatives, Ballmer has demonstrated himself to be a leader with a passion for innovation, entrepreneurship, and social responsibility.

As we reflect on Ballmer's life and work, there are numerous essential lessons we can draw from his example.

Lesson 1: Embrace Change

One of the fundamental characteristics that has made Ballmer so successful is his willingness to welcome change. Throughout his career, he has demonstrated a willingness to take risks, try new things, and adapt to changing situations.

From his early work at Microsoft to his recent charity initiatives, he has demonstrated a readiness to embrace change. Ballmer has been able to stay ahead of the curve and make a genuine difference in the world by remaining open to new ideas and techniques.

Lesson 2: Be Passionate

Another crucial lesson we may take from Ballmer is the value of enthusiasm. Throughout his career, he has demonstrated a deep devotion to the causes he believes in, whether it be technology, sports, or philanthropy.

This devotion has been visible in everything from his animated statements at Microsoft events to his enthusiastic ownership of the Clippers. Ballmer has been able to inspire others and make a significant influence on the world by bringing this level of passion to everything he does.

Lesson 3: Concentrate on People

Finally, one of the most important lessons we can take from Ballmer is the significance of focusing on people. Throughout his career, he has always placed people first, whether they are his employees, customers, or admirers.

This concern for people can be seen in everything from his attempts to enhance staff morale at Microsoft to his devotion to social justice and philanthropy. Ballmer has been able to develop solid relationships and have a positive effect on the globe by putting people first.

Uplifting words

As we look at Steve Ballmer's life and work, it is evident that he is a leader who has made a significant effect in the world. Ballmer has demonstrated himself to be a passionate and devoted leader who is driven to making a great influence on the world through his work at Microsoft, ownership of the Clippers, and philanthropic initiatives.

As we move forward, let us all aim to accept change, be passionate, and focus on people, as Steve Ballmer has done throughout his career. By doing so, we can all make a genuine impact in the world and leave a great legacy for future generations.

Printed in Great Britain
by Amazon

41832454R00036